# Copyright

# The Directors Coach

# On…

# Stakeholder Management

*"Not all Stakeholders are created equally…"*

A coffee time read

## About the Author

**David Miskimin** Accredited Fellow Coach IIC&M, MAC, Dip NMC

David is an accredited coach, consultant and trainer with extensive experience of working with Senior Executives, Directors, Board members and Senior Managers in the public, private and third sectors - in the UK and internationally. Activities additional to coaching are In-house Workshops – including the popular 'Ethics in the Workplace' and 'Strategic & Scenario Planning events'. He is an event speaker for conferences, seminars and meetings.

At the time of publication, he has delivered 6,500+ face-to-face coaching hours, through www.thedirectorscoach.com his coaching practice.

His approach is emergent and adaptive and he is particularly skilled in identifying conflicts between personal and organisational effectiveness.

His *Seminars and In-house Workshops* include:

- High Performing Teams
- Strengths Based Organisations
- Ethics in the Workplace
- Project Coaching
- Maximising Cultural Diversity in Teams
- Strategic and Scenario Planning
- Managing and Motivating

Clients select David for his *coaching* expertise in:

- Stakeholder Management
- Career/Talent Management and Transition
- Inspirational/transformational leadership
- Multicultural/virtual team development
- Fast growth and turnaround situations

David previously held positions including Major Account Management and Consultancy within ICL (Fujitsu), Reuters and Nortel. This period spanned 17 years.

David has strong UK and international experience, having run consulting, coaching and training projects with a range of organisations including Greenpeace International, NorthgateArinso, NHS, Seco Tools, EBRD, Iceland Foods, RBS, The Children's Society and Carphone Warehouse.

A popular speaker, he has appeared on BBC Radio Stoke, Merseyside and Manchester for interviews and phone-in coaching, and wrote a regular newspaper column for over 3 years.

Testimonials

*"David takes the time to understand what your goals are for the coaching to ensure that the desired outcomes are achieved. It was also encouraging to note in our first session that he had a real interest in the benefits to the organisation also and was keen to understand my line manager's perspective"* **Head of Corporate University, Financial Services**

*"His ability to draw upon a wide range of practical techniques and theories has measurably improved my confidence and ability to plan strategically. Yesterday a specific goal regarding the recruitment of a new team was fully met. What helped me achieve it was David's focus on clarifying my vision and making the right steps towards it"* **Director, National Charity**

*"David has had a fundamental impact on the business and its key personnel. Initially working with the top team on a one-to-one basis he brought each individual's personal goals and motivators into clear view. He then worked with the team as a new strategic plan was developed. The outcome was a clear set of objectives and a focus on what was going to have a real impact on the business.*

*Pet projects were axed if they didn't make commercial sense, responsibilities were delegated and steps put in place to communicate the new vision to the whole organisation.*

*His ability to handle the business aspects and personal ambitions/motivators of the key players was excellent. The result - a 50% increase in turnover and our best year ever... From being a player in the UK market we are well on the way to becoming the global niche specialist in our field. I would recommend David wholeheartedly to anyone wishing to make a positive change to their organisation"* **Chief Executive Officer, HR Software and Services Provider**

## Acknowledgements

Although I've two published books (www.thecoachingparent.com), for some time I've wanted to have a series of business books. Occasionally I 'played' with subjects, content and style. With a supportive push from my loving wife Laura, I committed to a topic which, for me, represents one of the fascinations when working in large organisations – 'Stakeholder Management'.

So several thousand words later a draft emerged. And there it sat as I continued to be distracted designing and delivering 1:1, group and team coaching – all things I love doing.

By now I suspect you will be detecting faint signs of procrastination in the author. As a coach who invites clients to reflect on 'what's working and what isn't' I knew my strengths in critical thinking and detail orientation were keeping me in a perfectionist trap. Questions like, 'how much content, ought there to be diagrams, how much detail is really needed?' and so on.

That's when Laura came to the rescue. *"Just design it as a coffee time read, or 30 minutes over lunch, don't over work it!"* Sound advice. Nothing like the one closest to you to tell it as it is!

A combination of an unexpected gap between projects and with this sage advice ringing in my ears provided the fuel and the essential focus needed to finish the work. A new goal was established, Laura and her razor sharp attention on typos and ambiguous narrative helping propel the work forward.

A big thank you to my clients for all the experiments you have boldly taken from our coaching together. Your feedback has been a source of great encouragement.

The biggest thank you again goes to Laura for your support, incision and love throughout.

If dear reader, you find any typos, or other errors in this work, it confirms the truth – this book was not produced by a robot, it is the output from a fallible human being! I hope you enjoy it.

**David Miskimin**

What good is it for a man to gain the whole world, and

yet lose or forfeit his very self?

**Luke 9:25**

## Contents

## Introduction

I decided to write 'The Directors Coach on…' series after thousands of hours delivering coaching, recognising certain themes repeatedly occurred and this meant they might just be important! I was keen to avoid producing a detailed academic study, having in mind a practical step-by-step approach to whatever the subject. Whether I've achieved my goal of a, simple to read, rapid to assimilate, and easy to remember approach will be down to you, the reader!

When working with senior individuals and teams I find the subject of 'Stakeholder Management' frequently comes up. The more senior the more likely it is to be a topic for discussion.

I suspect there are numerous reasons. One is a desire to have greater access to scarce resources through being more influential. Another is the trend towards matrix style organisations - which means it is becoming a more complex issue to manage. A third, and perhaps more obvious reason, is a lack of clarity over 'what exactly does 'Stakeholder Management' mean and why do I need to bother?' Once this has been understood, interest levels usually rise and consideration of identifying stakeholders can start.

The above reasons were the inspiration for this work. In the paragraphs below I'll explain the approach I will take in developing a strategy for Stakeholder Management.

When an initial list of stakeholders has been identified and recognised, you might wonder 'So now what?!' It is a key question because without consideration for the needs of these stakeholders progress will be limited.

Armed with a better understanding, contact approaches can now be planned and implemented.

Assuming a meeting, telephone discussion, or as a minimum an email, to set up an opportunity for the actual discussion, you need to plan how to convert all the preparation time and energy into a result and perhaps an ongoing business relationship.

## 1.  What is a Stakeholder?

I've found when discussing 'Stakeholders' no universal understanding exists. I would like to offer my simple definition:

*"A Stakeholder is an individual or group, with an interest in what you provide."*

So a Stakeholder is, in some way and for whatever reasons, interested in the product, project or service you produce, or perhaps the skills you offer or behaviours you exhibit.  For ease, throughout this work most times I will refer to 'service' or 'services'.

Stakeholder interest levels and attitudes towards you may vary.  They may be:

*Beneficial* - in that they are interested in a positive way about you and what you are doing

*Benign* – often a temporary state, as they have not yet established where you fit with their own Stakeholder

Management! They may be curious or indifferent if they have discounted your likely effect

*Belligerent* – whatever it is that you are doing, in some way has a negative impact or effect on the other party. Anticipate a response either direct or possibly indirect through their influence with others.

Given these different positions, it is essential to identify who your stakeholders are likely to be and why, potentially, they might have an 'interest'.

## 2. Why bother about Stakeholders?

If you are going to successfully influence your Stakeholders you must take time out to actually develop and build support. Theodore Roosevelt was reported to have said *"They don't care how much you know, they want to know how much you care."* Keeping this at the forefront of your mind when considering Stakeholders will ultimately serve you well.

Earlier I mentioned the 'matrix'. I'm not referring to the series of films, more an organisational structure that's cross-functional, cross-business group and other forms of interconnected working that cross the traditional vertical business units.

Many of my larger client organisations are moving, or have moved, towards a matrix structure. One of the difficulties of this arrangement is that individuals find themselves with multiple managers and encounter the different tensions that occur with this structure.

The theory behind a matrix structure is that an organisation will be able to respond with greater agility in today's fast moving market conditions. Given it's likely many of the Stakeholders that you will want to contact may face managing in a matrix structure, it will pay to give attention to which are the connection points of the matrix. In addition, you need to have a clear appraisal of your own skills in this environment.

The widely respected Hay Group undertook some research revealing that empathy, conflict management, self awareness and influence are essential qualities for leading in such an environment. Most strikingly the research reported all four of these qualities were found to be significantly lacking. I believe this makes it even more important for you, as you develop your Stakeholders, to understand your own, and your Stakeholders abilities in this context.

Not all Stakeholders are created equal. What I mean by this is its pointless building a massive network if the quality and range of your contacts is not wide or deep.

I encourage my clients to step outside their obvious areas of networking to add in expertise from other fields. In one instance I encouraged a group from a high tech engineering business to visit a social enterprise organisation. The learning exceeded all expectations as it became apparent that there were invaluable insights into the ways that issues could be dealt with via other organisations.

This leads to a paradoxical observation. Would it be a good idea to develop Stakeholder relationships without knowing if an individual could be a Stakeholder? There is something important about engaging with others generally which will assist self-awareness and empathy and influence. Who knows in a fast moving market how an individual in your network might become relevant as a future Stakeholder?

I am not advocating that everybody you target as a Stakeholder ought to be dealt in this way, what I am saying is to include a percentage of individuals that are not directly related to the task you have in hand.

While I am on the topic of paradoxical items, something else I've discovered and am pleased that Hay Group and others also confirm, is that those individuals who invest time in recording the results of their activities in a journal experience a by-product of creating greater space for enhancing their own self learning. As a result they accelerate through getting new perspectives which assist them in achieving their career objectives.

In exploring 'why bother?' let's consider what's good about bothering and what might be less good.

A realisation that every senior individual comes to is 'it's not possible to do everything myself'. This means you must harness the goodwill, talents and energies of others. To do this will take time and commitment to build both your own skills and the relationships that are necessary. The benefit of doing this is that by influencing in the right way, your likelihood of success and support for your proposals and initiatives increases exponentially.

Imagine you've submitted a proposal to your line manager for how your existing team needs to be restructured and perhaps enlarged. It's a terrific proposal, covers all the budgeting, timescales, resources, everything that is necessary. How can it fail?

When you then discuss your ideas with your manager you discover that it's not going ahead. Impossible you think - I've invested hundreds of hours on this document and it's a terrific idea for the business!

Perhaps you failed to discover that your manager talked to one of his peers about a possible restructuring event and your manager's peer, in some way, has influenced your manager not to go ahead with your ideas. How aware were you of this other significant Stakeholder and their interests? How aware were you that if you are employed by an organisation the relationship with your line manager is the single most important one? Failing to assess and manage it actively will inevitably lead to future issues.

So a downside of ignoring Stakeholders and not anticipating their needs is that there is often an unintended impact. The fact of not even anticipating this makes it all the more painful.

A downside of not assessing and understanding your Stakeholders means inevitable blind spots in our business proposals, worse is much wasted time, energy and unmet expectations in aiming to fulfil these objectives.

Ultimately, you will feel undervalued, simply because you haven't invested time in identifying and understanding your Stakeholders.

## 3. Identifying your Stakeholders

Working out who your Stakeholders are is a key task. It can also be confusing. Why - simply because Stakeholders usually occupy more than one category. As an example an individual may belong to a group. An organisation may also represent a group, e.g. A user group, yet there may be more than one organisation in a group, typically in a consortium.

Sometimes particular groups represent the interests of various consumers of your products or services. – E.g. Human Resources. Also as I've said, there may be consortia – those parties that have an interest in working with you, or that you need to persuade in favour of your approach.

Lets imagine you are preparing a bid to provide combined products and services to another organisation. For example, if you were working in the UK with the NHS as a potential client, a health service body might have an interest in Stakeholder groups that represent particular patient interests, the local education authority, perhaps the social services function.  Still feeling confused?  This simple diagram illustrates the contextual dilemma.

**Figure 1 – Stakeholder Categories**

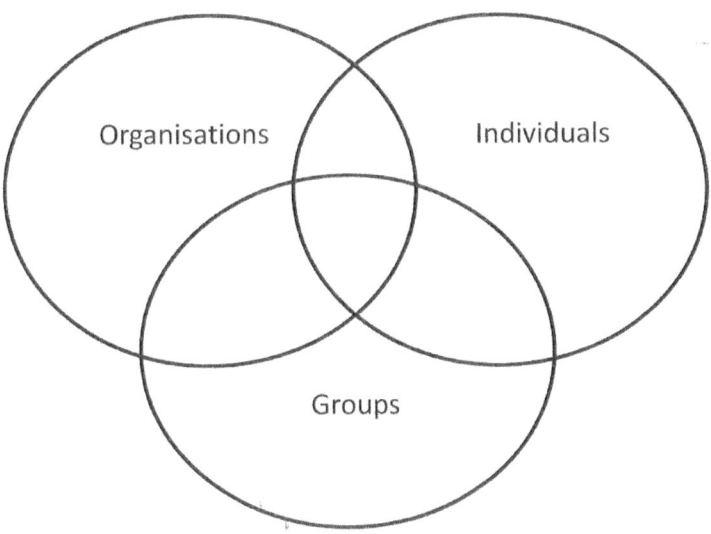

The above demonstrates the importance of identifying and then distilling groups and organisations down to individuals.  A reality is that every group has individuals who are more significant than other group members. An organisation is made up of individuals - which ones are the most influential?

Remember in making these personal judgements that deciding significance is relative purely to what you are offering. It doesn't matter that a person is important because of their role in an organisation. It does matter how they are affected by your offer.

Individuals, groups or organisations can be internal — within the organisation or, external — outside of the organisation. Note some category entries will appear under more than one heading. Examples for these categories include:

**Individuals**

- Colleagues
- Direct reports
- Line Manager
- Peers
- Various third parties

**Groups**

- Peers
- Clients/Customers
- The Community

**Organisations**

- Banks
- Clients/Customers
- Suppliers

These classifications, be they individuals, groups or organisations, need to be understood and influenced with integrity if you are to influence and ultimately achieve your business objectives.

Determining who exactly your Stakeholders are isn't necessarily as obvious as it might first seem. There are many things to take into account yet the most important one is, "what exactly do I want to achieve?" There can be different contexts that inform who your Stakeholders are.

Having considered the above, the immediate Stakeholders might now becoming clearer. They may well be your line manager, particular team members and then certain peers with whom you need to develop enhanced relationships. Outside of these groups will be others who are essentially indirect contacts. Those that you may occasionally bump into at networking events, conferences, some broader group activities.

Beyond these will be other, usually more senior individuals, that you would like to have access to, yet probably believe, are in some way, inaccessible or inappropriate to contact for your own particular grade or responsibilities.

My recommendation is that they all need to be considered, if only so that some can be eliminated as Stakeholders.

The best way to do this is to start analysing who exactly these individuals are and what it is that you have to offer them. Because of how well connected other individuals may be, there is an argument that not all Stakeholders are created equally. Some will be more important, more significant, depending on what it is you are wanting to achieve. This is going to require time, attention and focus. It may well also require an enhanced understanding of the power and politics that exist in any organisation of any size.

The next step is to invest time in analysing and mapping Stakeholders.

## Figure 2 – Stakeholder Analysis

| Who? | Why them? | Rating | Benefits of my services | Benefits to them Personally |
|------|-----------|--------|------------------------|----------------------------|
| Frank J | Line Manager! | +2 | Hits his target | Less hassle for him |
| | | | | |
| Sandra H | Peer | -3 | Joint target | Doesn't need to compete with me |
| John W | Ops Dir – senior influencer | +1 | Helps him spot rising talent | Succession planning concerns eased |
| etc. | etc. | etc. | etc. | etc. |

First consider *who* are your key Stakeholders and *why them*? There are a range of possibilities to start identifying and analysing individual Stakeholders, so this requires grabbing a piece of and building a hand drawn matrix paper <u>(See Fig. 2 - Stakeholder Analysis).</u> Later on you can turn this into a spreadsheet, document, whatever it is that works best for you, especially as you will be returning to it.

Now you have prepared an initial list consider – "how do I gauge the relationship at the moment?" It doesn't matter whether or not you've met the person or not at this point. We need to have a system of *rating* the relationship. Let's use a range between -5 to +5. To sharpen your assessment there will be no zeros permitted! What is a -5? Imagine you are standing at a bus stop with one of your Stakeholders. As the bus approaches this Stakeholder pushes you under the bus, that's a -5!

Now, rewind this uncomfortable picture. Imagine the bus is coming along and this time just as it arrives your Stakeholder says to you, "Let me jump under the bus for you". That's a +5!

Insert the person's name and relationship to you under the heading of 'Who' and 'Why Them?' Now add your initial 'Rating' of the relationship. Next consider what likely impact of whatever product or service you offer will have on this individual. In practical terms, what benefit is there in what you do?

Moving on to the heading of 'Benefits'. Split this into two parts. The first question is 'What business benefits does my service deliver – to them'. Next ask is "How does this individual *personally* gain from these benefit?" To assist imagine you are the other party and using the imaginary radio station adage 'WIIFM' – explore 'What's In It For Me?'

Investing time in understanding these related aspects, even if it's just guesswork at this stage, is going to help you at the later stage where you are going to check your Stakeholder's likely needs, when you are actually in contact.

It's important to remember this approach is focused on individuals. But you might be saying, "Well, I've got a group I need to address. How does this help?"

Remember, that groups are comprised of individuals. You'll need to identify that consortium, forum, whatever the title is, and start to break it down, not everybody in the group, simply focusing on that very small number who you assess as being influential within the group.  If you think about it, of all the different groups that you may know, ranging from your golf club, church, school, choir, tennis club, PTA – whatever it may be; you will know there are a small percentage who really are the ones that carry the major influence.  It's these that we are talking about.

Many years ago I was struck by the importance of acknowledging our interdependence on others.  It's easy to think, 'I've got a great service, so I can make this happen'; only to discover not everyone agrees, and even if you like each other, there may be no interest is your offering.

Don't be disheartened.  What's needed now is a method to build on your initial analysis and categorise Stakeholders and this is where <u>Figure 3 – Stakeholder Mapping</u> will assist.

## Figure 3 – Stakeholder Mapping

(Acknowledgements to the work of P. Block)

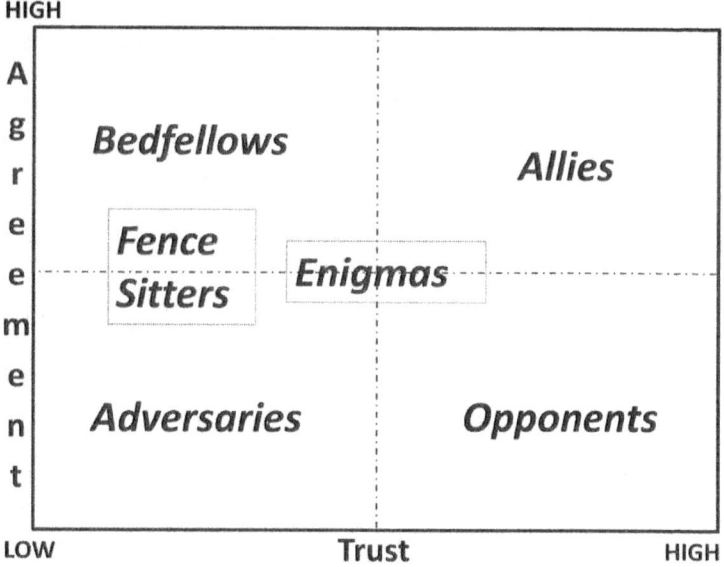

*Understanding the Stakeholder Mapping diagram:*

**Trust**: To what extent can we rely on the stakeholder's support for this initiative?

**Agreement**: To what extent might we agree about likely benefits of the project, or service?

Before examining different combinations of agreement and trust as defined above, consider your intentions and any prior history:

- Who the person is
- Frequency/quality of dialogue to date
- How well relationship is developed

Having asked yourself the above questions, the next action is to assess where this person might be in relation to agreement and trust - relative to whatever it is you will be offering:

High Agreement / High Trust: *Allies*

People who share our vision and want us to succeed. When we meet, communication is open, honest and authentic. They frequently enthuse about our vision, and support flows naturally and spontaneously. People with whom we are comfortable being vulnerable.

Action: Lobby this category the most. Consider discussing the relationship and your agreement about the benefits. Discuss shared doubts and seek advice and support. Invite them to promote the benefits of your services to others.

### High Trust / Low Agreement: *Opponents*

People who do not share our vision, disagreeing with our purpose, direction and goals. However trust is high because they are clear, authentic and genuine in their communication with us.

Action: Consider the perceived quality of the relationship, and state your own position on the service. Ask for their perception on their position. Explore shared problem solving.

## High Agreement / Low Trust: *Bedfellows*

People who are in agreement with us but in whom we have a low to moderate level of trust. When we have contact with them we are more watchful and careful about what and how we communicate.

Action: Consider affirming agreement on the benefits. Acknowledge reasons for why caution may exist.  Be very clear about what you'd like in terms of working together. Ask what they want from you and explore if agreement is possible.   Keep checking will they actually follow through on any agreements?

## Low Trust / Unknown Agreement: *Fence Sitters*

People who simply will not take a stand either for or against. Interpersonally excellent to the extent that they seldom, if ever offend, but rarely commit.

One of the most important things about fence-sitters is their numbers - they are often in the majority.

Action:  Work hard to convert them to your viewpoint. Fence-sitters are often in the majority, so given their likely higher numbers the more you can convert the greater the chance of success.

Low Trust / Low Agreement: *Adversaries*

People who were possibly Bedfellows or Fence Sitters, but with whom negotiation has failed. People who take up our energy.

Action:  Much time can be wasted to persuade this group of the brilliance of your offering.  A much better tactic is in moving away from focusing on those who aren't accepting us, and rather, investing time and effort in those who are supporting or those who haven't made up or announced their view yet – Fence-sitters and Enigmas in particular.  Don't invest heavily in trying to persuade them around to your way of thinking.  Do, identify those in other 'matrix positions' who are in favour of you and who also may be in a position to talk with your Adversaries.

## Unknown Trust / Unknown Agreement: *Enigmas*

You haven't yet got a clue as to where they stand on this particular project! That's because in many ways Enigmas are the hardest to deal with. Enigmas have a knack of flying under the radar.

Action: If struggling to get an Enigma's input, the best thing you can do is to sound out colleagues about what has helped them in the same situation. Keep conversation focused on the work itself and test out what you perceive are the benefits for this type.

Now that you have analysed and mapped your stakeholders, there are different ways to use the data.

I suggest a good way to start is to simply place the initials of the person into the matrix and include your rating alongside. Now you need to test your awareness of your Stakeholders by asking yourself some questions:

1. What financial or emotional interest do they have in the outcome of your work?

2. What do they need from you?

3. How is your reputation with them and what is the evidence for that?

4. Who influences their opinions?

5. Is it necessary to add any of these opinion influencers to your Stakeholders analysis?

6. For those who are less supportive what benefits might win them around?

7. If you don't think you can win them around, how will you manage their opposition?

8. If someone is rated at +5, is that person really an enthusiastic advocate?

9. How can I have leverage from the strengths i.e. the high positive ratings?

10. Which negative ratings can I safely ignore?

11. If I've rated someone as -5, is that person a major impediment? Will that person work actively to block my support or proposals?

12. If I've rated someone as +1, will they definitely at least go along with my proposals?

13. If I've rated someone as -1, will that person at least stay out of the way?

14. Who could I involve to help me?

15. What exactly am I going to do and by when?

Answering these questions helps test the quality of your data and whether they are correctly positioned on your matrix. Have you really made sure you have made the fullest assessment of allies, opponents, adversaries, and bedfellows? Perhaps share your findings with a trusted other to help calibrate the details. Failure to do so will likely lead to a lot of wasted time and effort.

In conclusion while recognising the political aspects of business I decided this work would not attempt to address in depth the politics and underlying drivers and games played. In using the methods described so far I have highlighted some methods of assessing those relationships that exist within organisations.

## 4. Anticipating your Stakeholders likely needs

Have you ever been in a situation, usually in a meeting, where you felt "I wish I'd done more preparation beforehand?" Usually by anticipating your Stakeholder's likely needs you increase the probability of being more influential and memorable in the meeting.

Let's say you've decided an individual is likely to be valuable to meet. In this case some research is essential. There are many sources of information, the Internet being an obvious one. If you research using any of the popular search engines, then you will find mostly at no financial cost, social media offers plenty of insights from blogs and articles, to specialist interest groups and conversation threads. These may be on Twitter, Facebook, Linkedin, Pinterest, etc,. of the many sources available.

If you work with or for an organisation there may be an agreed or prescribed social media approach with Yammer, Socialcast or another enterprise based social networking/knowledge sharing tool.

More traditionally it's worth asking others, "Do you know anything about this individual, if so what might you tell me?" Make sure you understand these perceptions to further inform the approaches you might bring to the table.

In undertaking this research, examine some of the timelines e.g.:

- How long has this individual been in the organisation?
- Where were they before?
- What roles have they held?
- Is there an obvious career path, or is it quite eclectic?

In doing this also notice your own path. Does yours in any way mirror any of the activities the individual has been, or is, involved in? This will become more relevant in Chapter 6 - At the Stakeholder meeting.

When you consider the role of this person, how much do you actually know about their agenda, their role, what their function actually entails? You don't need to become an expert, however it's worth researching some of the things that could be included in the role, once again, the internet is a great source of ideas. If you were looking at the details say of an Operations Manager, then searching for CVs, job specifications, objectives of Operations

Managers, will actually give you further specific information. This will come from job notice boards, from academic papers, from CVs that individuals have placed on the internet (not always knowingly either, as internet indexing can produce some surprising data!).

Now you can begin to wonder what some of the possible concerns of the Stakeholder might be. We could discover that an Operations Manager is interested in how the different functions interrelate with each other, often that's about process and the flow of data between departments.

Coming up with ideas at this stage are essential in identifying how the various aspects of anticipating needs will influence your approach when you get to the Stakeholder meeting.

Identifying the above will help you focus on the topic for the next chapter - "How exactly am I going to approach them?"

## 5. Contacting Stakeholders

Now that you have identified your key Stakeholders and undertaken some initial work in anticipating their likely needs, it's important to get a meeting arranged. It's a matter of personal choice as to whether this will be by email, social media, telephone, even working on a chance meeting so that you might request a get together. Our aim here is to get a one-to-one meeting. Targeting of Stakeholder groups requires different approaches.

The focus at this point is about adding value, being professional and efficient. This means your request is to arrange a meeting of "up to 20 minutes". This will become significant as you progress this interaction. You need to communicate what exactly it is that you are offering in having a meeting. You also have to consider what it is you are asking for, which at this point is 20 minutes of someone else's time. It's purely an initial investment of time together and will be by nature, exploratory. So, what might this look like if it were, for example, an email or a telephone conversation?  I offer an option below:

*"I'm currently developing my business network and believe it will be to our mutual benefit to invest in a short meeting of not more than 20 minutes together.  This would very much be exploratory and I would anticipate sharing some of the areas on which I am currently working.*
*These include…*

Note, here you need to mention one or more areas of what you believe are potentially shared interests, informed by your research following on from Chapter 4 - Anticipating your Stakeholders likely needs.

*If you are amenable to this approach, I propose to make contact with your office during the coming week."*

In summary, this is a clear and concise email or telephone message.  It has a particular constructive approach with a mutuality proposed.  Also, it provides for the option for the individual to respond either indicating their amenability or lack of it.

An alternative approach which can be successful, depending on both yours and your target Stakeholder's operating methods, is to use social media. I have received requests from individuals where in social media they have asked would I be prepared to introduce them to somebody I already know.

One of the benefits of social media is it often indicates who will be in my networking circle. Of course, the same is true in reverse. It's possible, if someone uses social media, for you to observe other contacts that may potentially give you access to your Stakeholder.

I certainly have used this, not just in the UK but also with individuals who are overseas. And provided the reason to make contact is in the 'potential value I am offering you', then most times the referrer (i.e. the person who already knows you), will be comfortable introducing you to another party who, at this stage, is unknown to you.

It's very much about being open and reasonable with your request for contact. So, as an example, you might say to your referrer,

*"I notice that person x is in your network, I have some information regarding Operations Management that I think will be of interest to them. Would you be prepared to refer me to them via Linkedin, Facebook etc?"*

Remember, if you've done sufficient work in the identification of the Stakeholder and anticipating their needs, at this point you should have more than enough information that you could share with the referrer in order to encourage the likelihood that they will put you forward.

## 6. At the Stakeholder meeting

Some meetings with Stakeholders will be one-off, many will not. From your perspective the main purpose of having the meeting is often so you can create a bridge head to developing the initial contact into an ongoing mutually beneficial relationship – See <u>Chapter 7 - Developing the initial contact into an ongoing business relationship</u>.

Given this, what is the minimum reason for the Stakeholder meeting? Well, its aim is to establish credibility – and that's a two-way process, part of your own qualification about the relationship is an implied question; 'How credible is the individual I am meeting with?' In other words, are they likely to be a good future source that is worth nurturing?

Unfortunately, it is the case that sometimes you will conclude, well that was a useful meeting, however I won't be investing in developing it any further. It's during this meeting that you are going to establish how well did you anticipate your Stakeholder's likely needs.

See <u>Chapter 5 -Anticipating your Stakeholders likely needs.</u>

Going into the meeting, my recommendation is that you have in your mind a set of targets. These would be a 'minimum target', in other words, I really mustn't leave the meeting without having established this. There needs to be your 'best target', so this is what you would consider to be ideal and worthwhile.

Lastly, have a 'bonus or stretch target'. Sometimes it happens in a meeting that you quickly achieve all the things that you thought were possible and then realise, after having left, 'I could have asked for this, I could have checked that'. Don't fall into that trap, have an absolute fantasy bonus that you can ask for, or discuss, when everything else has been achieved. I have found it remarkable how often these bonuses actually come to reality.

When you were doing your earlier research, this is now the time to check in with some of your understanding.

Starting with some context is always a good idea. 'How does the Stakeholder see the current business climate? What are their top three priorities at this time? And, most importantly, what would they like to get out of this interaction the two of you are having?' This is referred to as "seeking first to understand, then be understood", and there are several sources, paraphrases and adaptations for that philosophy.

Another factor to consider in the meeting is, how exactly are you going to add value so that the person you are meeting with appreciates you are somebody valuable to know, somebody who would be worth having a future interaction with.

This is where any wider research will be helpful. You may want to mention, 'I happen to have noticed in e.g. the field of operations that ['item of interest'] happens, how does that relate to your own function?' Now the Stakeholder appreciates that you have invested time, they may well feel more valued. You could in that moment also provide some specific information in a field of specialism that interests them. It may be something that, if subsequently used by them, enhances their credibility.

All of these things are increasing your influence and with integrity. I do not advocate manipulation, or insincerity as a tactic of influence. Your genuine intent needs to be one of serving the other person first by understanding their needs and then adding value in so that they recognise your part. It's very much a testing and discovery process. You may want to think of it as a form of due diligence.

Embedded within your whole approach is an honest intention to establish rapport with each other, that's a harmonious state where it's comfortable to share ideas and offer information and suggestions. I have noticed that some individuals will feel uncomfortable with this approach, and vulnerable with this style in an initial meeting. However, my experience is that the quicker this occurs the more successful the meeting will be and the likelihood of both parties outcomes being met, enhanced. A personal discovery you are likely to make here is that the preparation, however complete, in anticipating your Stakeholder's likely needs is now being fully exposed.

In leaving the meeting, we need to be aware that the aim is to turn this initial contact into an ongoing relationship which we will discuss in the next chapter.

## 7. Developing the initial contact into an ongoing business relationship

Some time ago I listened to an article by international speaker Roger Dawson where he argued that the "value of a service always appears to go down quickly as soon as those services have been performed".

Those of you who have provided some form of service to a client, organisation or even to somebody you just know well, realise that this is true. There's a fairly rapid decay between appreciation and something just becoming matter of fact. This effect is important when you recognise the aim is to move from an initial contact into an ongoing relationship.

It is the case that some relationships are likely to be more valuable than others and, in a two-way process, each party will be deciding what perceived value is involved in the interaction and what it might offer for the future. So it is really important to understand where this initial contact stands and how to position it.

There are two parts that I tend to consider here. One is in the immediate, where you've had the meeting and now it's about closing it off. This is not so difficult. As the meeting draws to an end you might enquire, "It's been great to meet with you, how has that been for you?" And whatever their response, you must ask, "Was there anything of particular value in what we've considered?" This will give you a clue as to where there may be a hook or something else that you can follow through with.

At this point there will either be an immediate agreement i.e. 'Lets meet again in a couple of months', or whatever it is depending on the way the conversation has gone, alternatively it will be left more open. So you are just establishing the principle of continuity. The conversation here goes something like, "I'm glad it's been of value, will it be okay if I come back to you in a few months .....?"

By leaving the timeframe open you will get a sense from the response. It will either be "Yes that's fine", something more specific e.g. "Let's make it six", or "Can we leave it for the moment?" So, the first two are great at this stage. Your aim is to turn this initial contact into an ongoing relationship. That's quite different from an individual saying "Well I'm not sure what would be the point of a future meeting", in which case you've not achieved your objectives. So, best to close on that note and move to the next stage.

This is where time becomes important. As I've said earlier, the value of what you've delivered in the meeting will diminish rapidly so you need to have ways of continuing the relationship between now and the interval. None of this needs to be high maintenance; however it does need to be planned.

Some people like to use a simple reminder system. This could be via an online calendar, could be in your diary, it may be you've got something on a Smartphone or similar. Make an entry at the agreed time or perhaps a week ahead of the agreed time.

So if you've agreed to follow up in three months, then after 11 weeks an entry in the diary 'follow up due, individual X'. More immediately, within a week maximum of your initial meeting, send an email or it could be a text, perhaps a newspaper cutting that you saw; whatever it is that you find, send it to the individual with the line "saw this and thought of you".

It doesn't need to be more than that as long as it has your name on it. This individual knows you are giving attention to their needs and you've focussed in on something they've said. Your task is finding something in those seven days. That means referring to the internet, a newspaper you read, or chatting with other people.

The reason you are doing the above is to turn your investment of time into a shared investment in the future. Your concentration is on adding value. Your intention is to confirm key things that were discussed and, more importantly, needed and for you to maintain the relationship. The interesting thing in this behaviour is you'll start to become much more aware of the needs of others, which in itself is a good thing!

## 8. In Closing

I hope the step by step approach described has inspired you in deciding to better manage your Stakeholders. I've found over the years that having a consistent and clear method definitely makes a difference. It's also respectful, as implicitly you will be acknowledging the other party.

The good news is that by taking a detailed approach you can use the opinions of the most powerful stakeholders to shape your projects at an early stage. This makes it more likely they will support you and their input may improve the quality of your project.

I've already said scarce resources are an issue for senior individuals. The reverse of this is gaining support from powerful Stakeholders can help you to win more resources e.g. internal resources, which makes it more likely your projects will succeed.

You can ensure Stakeholders know what you are doing and fully understand the benefits of your project by communicating early and often.

Inevitably there is much more that could be said and I suspect you will have your own thoughts, ideas and variations.  By all means let me know, through the Contact Us page on the website below, and I will happily consider including them and the source in a future edition.

**David Miskimin**

**The Directors Coach**

**www.thedirectorscoach.com**

PS – Would you like me to let you know when the next *'The Directors Coach on…'* becomes available?  If so, once again, contact me through the Contact Us page on the website above and I'll gladly put you on the wait list.  If my writing style 'works for you' and there is another business topic you'd like it would be great to hear from you.